MW01615055

eat me.

drink me.

be me.

We are not the Alice in Wonderland
but the Wonderland in Alice.
Not a character with a role to play
but a Place where play happens.

wave ones

WHERE LOVE IS MADE

Something grows
Tired of
Forgetting and
Falls down
A hole
Into a bed
That is
Made of
Remember.

There
We
Make
Love.

•

To dis-solve ***eat me,*** actually:

Nothing just happened.
Nothing is about to.
T h i s is what is happening.
Haaaaaaaaaaaaaaa...
Let it be.
Soften so so so much Into this
moment.
Aaaaaaaaaaah...
There is nothing you need.
Aaaaaaaaaaaaaaaaaah...
Softening the eyes.
Softening the belly.
Softening the heart.
Letting go.
Completely.
Again.

•

If you would now, wherever the wave of your existence
might be expressing its distinction at this moment,
consider slightly turning upwards the corners of your lips
allowing the eyes to s o f t e n, the heart to s s s s s h ,
and the mind to m e l t for this moment so you might
resemble the sea and
find yourself reflected.
Here, there is nothing for you to believe.
Nothing here to ponder.
Take this in with your heart. Let it softly consider itself
then let it go along with everything else you can think of.
If just for this moment.
For truth truly cannot be thought.
Only d i r e c t l y e x p e r i e n c e d . ∞

•

Drop Story.

Nowhere to be. No one to be. No one not to be.

S h a d o w B o x i n g -

If we were handed a transcript of our subconscious thoughts, we'd be shocked by all the shadow-boxing. Mind is trying to figure out what other people think of us, and then defending our position against what we think they think of us-
We can take off the gloves. We needn't know! We can't know. And engagement of the mind in this activity is brutal.

•

Our defending against shadows gets in the way of being who you'd have them think you are, anyway! We can become aware of our subconscious thoughts. Walk in on them. Catch them in the act. Like children who are wrestling, they will stop because an adult has entered the room.
So be of witness. A compassionate and loving parent. Sssssssssh, you say. Get up, I made some cookies.

B r e a t h combs the field

So we can

P l a y .

∞

•

• A N Y • W O R D •

The rookie angel says to the elder,

' They seem so much confused. Why not tell them? '

' They are too so much inside the head. Any word, no matter how true, is bait further into their trap. '

' And so what do we do? '

' We l o v e . '

' And wait? ' asks the rookie.

' And wait. '

Thinking the mind out of thinking is like trying to wash a window with a dirty cloth.

dis · solve -

Draw the fever down from the head.

Any resistance is only fuel to the fire.

Mind cannot drive out mind.
Only heart can do that.

((so much softening into it))

Stop.

Sound this out.

"Mmmmmmmmm"

Freedom is the opposite of the enslavement of right and wrong, good and bad, black and white. The idea that there is a right answer and, alternatively, a very wrong answer is a symptom of a mind enslaved.

Now the mind will inevitably offer these ideas. Not believing it is

l i b e r a t i o n .

Allowing for huh, a letting go, a... r e l a x a t i o n .

And relaxation in itself is also the tool to become free, letting go to access liberation. S u r r e n d e r i n g .

M U D

I am a wet
Dog
Shaking off ego
Constantly
So I can roll
Around in the
Dirt
Without getting

Stuck.

•

OFFERING

What else
For you
Can be
Offered
When you are the
Offering?
And what else
Would we offer
But the best
Which is you
And everything?

So I offer it all,
Love,
And trust you
To take care of
Yourself.

•

A L C H E M I S T R Y -

Gratitude is love entering the body in whatever form and, if not clung to, exiting the body, as gratitude.

Pain comes through the body and if not clung to, held onto, identified with, it passes through the body and comes out as forgiveness.

Success held becomes fear. Allowed, it becomes humility. Humility is love.

Forgiveness, gratitude, success and fear – words of human accounting. Their only existence is in the physical world.

•

And pain is obstructed love.

Pain is the flow that comes out of the obstruction of F l o w . The obstruction itself, the pain, held onto, is the obstruction of love – again. A pain spiral.

If allowed through, however, if allowed to flow, pain emerges as forgiveness and is transmuted into love. It is love. It is all one huge flow of love. Constantly being asked to just be allowed to come through. To not be held in the quality it was received, congealed as whatever quality it was received, just to be allowed. Let it through. And in doing so, constantly open to receive whatever is Next,

N o w, and in doing so constantly let go the non-essential, maximize receptivity and output of the Flow, the A l l - the Essence That You Are .

TENTH SHEEP

There is nothing to hold onto. Give all of yourself away. So much we are trying to seem okay, seem successful, seem happy... we try to show, project a certain image. And we hold on so tightly all of the "If they saw this, I would not be loved." Or even, if I see this I will not love myself... We hold back. We hold on.

A flock of sheep walks under a shepherd's rod. As they pass under, they are counted and the tenth is the Offering. It is to be given up in its entirety, to be drawn close to the All. Of that sheep it is said: "It is not up to you to search it or check it. To deem whether it is worthy or not. To weigh in on it as good or bad, perfect or imperfect, fat or thin, intelligent or dumb, speckled or sparkling.

It is the one that is wanted. Wholly."

It is said that every human soul is the tenth sheep.

It is not for you to hold on and say: "This part is not good enough, I will hide it away. I should be different. This part is not ready yet. This part was dumb all along!"

You are the one that is wanted. You are the tenth sheep.

It is not for you to hold back and say: "Wait, I am not ready, that is not good, that is not beautiful, they will not love me... "

There is nothing for you to hold onto. There is all of you to offer, without even knowing what it is.

The mind is analyzing the soul on its way through to portals of your cells, saying, wait that one's missing a part, that one's not ready for shipment, that one's just emBArrasing - Mind is not the boss of you. ALL of it is wanted. It is not up to you to hold it back, to inspect it or exchange it. No inspection. Surrender. The perfect offering that you are. And in that letting go we are reabsorbed with the All. The little idea of who we thought we were, the goods the bads, the shoulds, the diets, all, reabsorbed into the maximum embodiment. Of Being. Simply Being.

Even that, the, oh my, we're not even doing this right because I AM inspecting, analyzing every move.. the next sentence says, " and if you DO inspect and exchange it for another, BOTH are holy." Even when you DO analyze a moment and your perfect heart to death, even the moment that you've squandered is perfect. And so, aaaaaaaaah, this too is perfect. Every "But-" the mind can say- yes, that too is holy, perfect, wholly perfect. Letting go. Softening into all that you are.

Silence Says -

There are very few things that Silence says.
Mostly, not surprisingly, it's silent.

But sometimes, that "Peace That Passes Understanding"
understands
We want to hold it
Crystallizes down to a gem, pressing into the palm of your mind saying,
"Meet me later."

Saying, "Take this, for when your mind takes over. It has the power to lead you back to me. My room key."

There are words silence says that are hall passes Back - having come out the concert door, directly.

I'm a radical substitute teacher, unruled (like lined paper) by the principal, overruled by the principle of giving freely a
pass to any soul brave enough to Ask . So they can set their wonder to

Wandering.

•

"Thank G ∞ d we don't exist."
and
there
it is. we.
at
Constant
Climax

Silence is not what it sounds like.

S O F T N E S S

It is forever and always our
S o f t n e s s at stake.

It's the wine the whole earthly vessel embraced.
Condensed as a chalice chiseled just to hold s p a c e .

My L o v e , it is your essence
In the presence of
This
M o o n .

It is the part that is remembered
when noise, annoyed by sister S i l e n c e,
Leaves the room.

The silence comes in many out-fits of rage,
Madness and scorn. It ducks under confusion, addicts you to porn.
Meanwhile, it's holy as the day you were born.

•

AWESTRUCK

A shadow has been to the west of me.

Now it is east!

There must have been time
Where
No Shadow
Was.

And I was too busy striking twelve, to know.
Erect, exalted, exalting,
Aligned.

Oh, You!
Tell!
Will i ever know Y/our Face?

•

ALL STRING THINGS

Maybe it is that we
Go in and out of life
A needle pulling
Thread through
A foundation,
Making
Something
In and out
Through to the other
Side makes the
Mark.
You've made a mark
Linear looking, by going
All up and down-like.
From beneath it is shaggy,
All string things -
Disconnected.

There has been a glimpsing,
Though, from just above
Hover up.
The Hand pulls and we
Get to go in the
Non-knowing Place.

The seeing no
Longer with i,
But the
Eye
Of the needle
Without
Need.

Breath(e).

Plunged down beneath.

Again.

And maybe the death
Is a description time,
Like this.
When words come
Back
That were snatched
When in sight flight took the
Breath Away.

Speechless.

Darkness brings all
Vibration
To note
To throat
Out
Let.

The She you think you'd
Seen,
The One you Know
You'd Been.
The Tapestry revealed
And
- gasp -
your moment above
when the moment
consciousness
asked
"Who are you and Who
shall I say sent
me?" A souvenir,
please,
so I know I was
here, and oh where,
how to come again
this near.

Swallowed again, and
All was clear
- inarticulably -
plunged down, again
beneath the tapestry.

Full of string theories,
song and philosophies.

Yours is the
Death
Shown to me.

The death of You,

Into me.

I am your coffin, truly,
Dear G ∞ d.
This body holds,
Some afterglow

And that lifeforce
Bid I to
Flower some
Prose of

And How
When We
As One,
Arose.

A s c e n d .

WORDS SERVE

Words serve
You
Until the
Trays are
Empty
So they run
Back to the
Kitchen
Anxious
(Only to serve)

To find
Nothing More
So they stick
Their heads
In the oven
And we eat them
As offering
And there is
Silence.

That Day Came.

•

Melt into me.

- ∞

Every cell be a lover's mouth
These of this
Body
Lock
Kiss
Permeating
Penetrating air.
Inside the moment I plunge
Masculine
Deep.
I pierce through
Sky's shy
Passivity
Crown off.
It's mutual.

On my knees.

No more- *please*
Sweet succulent
Juice.

Eye pierce through
Waters above
Sky
Divide
Red sea
Bleeds
Lifeblood
Out me.
I land on back
I am torn open
All

I am that I am

Ecstasy is a word
Unpacked and
Empty
Here are no moods
But only
Here
This room
This
Room
Is the one
All houses are built
And torn
Down
Within
We live here.
We are
Here and nothing

Else.
We are the house
Boundless and taller

Than alice
It cannot be filled.
Orgasm aspires
Ecstasy
Bliss
Play games
Of pretend
They cannot match
The face of this
Place.
Nightmares are dust
In corner
That sun dances with

Making snow flake
You are the kingdom
Ego is a curtain
Falling backwards
Through placeless
Space
Into yourself.
Myself.
Same
No
Thing.

Aaaaah.

•

GAME OVER

The Good Fight
Is the ego's struggle
In this life.

She wins
Everytime

She forfeits
To Soul.

•

F . O . A .

Can you IMAGINE if
This pizza,
Can you IMAGINE if
These (wo)men,
These flowers my mind picks,
Were my
Truest desires?
Can you IMAGINE if
My heart
Weren't
Full On Arrival
And the palette
Of this soul
Had any cravings
But the
Love
That is made
Freshly
Every atom
Of moment?
My tongue is a
Funny simulation of
The buds below
And blossoms ideas

To be swallowed
Constantly
Sent to the depths of being.
That takes it in saying
Mmmmmmmmmm
Mmmmmmmmm
mmmmmmmm...
It is absorbed into
All
Automatically
Without question
Without action
With
Compassion, only-

Reception
Of
All.

Nothing
Can stir the stomach of
G∞d.

•

When the me is traded for the
I am, she never looks back
in regret.
She is busy
Basking in the light of who she's
become.
"Me" is a speck on the windshield
of the i am.
in moments she wishes
she were driving,
but mostly she is
head back squealing
at the inconceivable
joy
of this ride.

∞ JUST DESSERTS ∞

'Wait'
While fully
Gathered and full,
For the next meal.
It will come.
Or not.
It is all
Dessert.

•

N O T H I N G LEFT

There is nothing left to wear
There is nothing left to eat
There is nothing left to say
Y o u are worn and never ware
Words are eaten and
Fullness I s .

•

∞

KEEPING A SECRET

Everyday I feel
Is my
Birthday
And I am not telling
Anyone.
I am keeping a secret
That if they knew

They
Would
Sing.

•

Immediately seeing into this new N o w , we are alive and unscathed. We are born new and now. today.

You • F R E S H E S T Little C U P C A K E • You !

The world is
A party of people who saw
You very drunk
Last Night.
Best to show up, today,
This Moment
As a
First meeting,
' Hello!
Wonderful to be here! '
With not-a-once searching out glimpse of
What they know of you
' Before-' without a hesitance of ' Do you find me despicable?
Did I spill wine down your dress? Do you k n o w me, or...'
A secret: when you know nothing is your business,
everything becomes your Play, your passion, a vacation day.
Analysis is doomed. What you see in every eye has
NOTHING to do with you 99.9% of time.
Sweep the crumbs of yesterday into the freshest
Cupcake
Now.
You are new.
Handshake whole.

Happy Birth-Moment!
I am open to
Pain, Joy,
N o w .

•

W E B O U N C E

There is the universal layer of being, in which we are all
Each
Other.
i admit a preference to that O n e , if even as a source-point from which to P l a y .
The constant couch we jump from, now now now.
Too fun to stop, even when we be warned we will get hurt. -
We dooo.
And get back up .
Trusting the couch, itself,
Resilience is ours.
We
Bounce back.

•

When we flow forgiveness fully, within,
we find no self there to be forgiven.
We find that we *fully* are the forgiveness itself.

RESCUING MIRRORS

How can we show one
His own greatness?
Only by mirroring it
And holding his
When he slips.

Love and love and love.
There is nothing to fix
But to l o v e .

And so much more to love
Than to
Do.

•

IN IT (Unconditional Love)

I love all
Who cannot
Love me
When I show
Imperfection.
That is their
Imperfection
And in it
I love them.
Even when I can't.
Thereby I can love me
Even when i
Am empty.
Love is love is
Love.

•

There is no condition to our being.
There is nothing to think, do, say, know, be.
We are, unconditionally. We are what is there steadfastly under all of our trying, doing, calculating, posturing, helping, describing, manipulating and apologizing.
What is there. Here.
Now.

FIRST DAY

The Known
Is a Babysitter
Whose leg we
Will not let GO
Of.
She is trying to do her duty in
Dropping us the hell OFF on our
Very
First
Day.

We've got no IDEA
That our Mother's the
One waiting inside the
School wondering what's
Keeping us.

Oh the wonders she wants to teach.

Oh, let the
Unknown
Undo
You.

Lie down, baby.
Mama's gonna show you
The way life is when you

Stop clinging anxiously
To ankles.

Mama's gonna show you the view from
Within.

•

STILL

Time moves. I am still.
The body moves. I am still.
The mind
Moves. I am
Still.
She dies. I am still.
He dies. I am still.
I die. I am still.

Yes, still.

I still am.

•

Your destiny is the last idol in your temple.

It Is

Everything
That is so
Total
It includes
Even
Nothing

Emptiness
That is so
Full
It includes
Everything.

•

I love you.

Love,

Y o u .

(∞)

i am the hand that pulls the string
i am the dreaded, happy thing,
i am undone by all that is i.
i am what happens in the blink of an eye

i am the i that knows no we
so dissolved this duality.

the we that knows no i.
die into me as we lift our eyes.

•

YOU SAID

"My favorite poem I ever heard."
- Eckhart Tolle

"Her words are alive the same way notation can fly off a page and become sweet music."
- Jason Mraz

"Of the same wealth and value as anything one can hope to find in a volume of Rumi, Hafiz, St. John of the Cross, or St. Teresa of Avila. A grand range of mind and soul awaits any who ventures near Alice Frank's verse. Her poems can help us defy gravity. Who doesn't trade their gold for that?"
- Daniel Ladinsky

Directions from this book:

(Sometimes when you go for your phone,
reach for me, instead.)

•

my real name is

Y∞U

ISBN 978-1-60280-317-6

Print year 2018 (N o w .)

Published by
KTAV Publishing House
527 Empire Blvd.
Brooklyn, NY 11225

Phone 718-972-5449
Fax 718-972-6307
www.ktav.com
orders@ktav.com

Interior illustration and design
by Farshid Shafiey
Cover art and design by Jon Marro
Book design by Alice Frank

B'H

I know you are but what i am.

- ∞.

Nothing just happened.

Nothing is about to.

THIS

is what is

happening

•

L I G H T .

Light is a particle and a wave.
Most things are either, or.
Light is *and.*

That is what makes it light.

Much like light- As light, this human experience
of each day, each moment, falls somewhere along a
spectrum of being particle or wave.

Some days more p a r t i c u l a r, more human, with
edges.
Some days more wave, more universal and formless,

At One.

•

particle poems

2 D L V R -

Hey you, little google man. You cannot catch me with your RAM. Take a little hinternet, your tweets don't wet my pinterest. Because you're a face pulled on a screen that says your name, your likes, your dreams.
But we are worth kagillion pixels. We take more memory than all of facebook's pictures. I want my ear to tickle with sweet breath's whispers. To be the ones we're waiting for, let's be love up in this place. Be 3D, or even more! Let's throw in all our words for love, and show up as its
Face.
A 2D lover is agony.

Okay, your texts are really sweet, but they're still not saying where to
Meet.
So you're the master of the daily haiku,
But you're all thumbs until you show Y o u . Eat your words or waste me. They're no good until you taste me.
You can't scrape the sky with a map of the Big Apple. Go through withdrawal seeing someone's tracks. Your adam's app won't say a thing until you've been to where you're being.

Have you been to where you're being?

I'm so glad you came to my door. Your glow was
So.
Worth.
Waiting.
For.
Hearing you feel me audibly. This love is so much
better than technology. Brighter than verizon sun,
your soul samsungs my HTC one.
Because You are worth kagillion pixels. Let's
Make more memories than all of facebook's pictures.
You tickle my ear with sweet breath's whispers. Being
the ones we're waiting for, we get to be love up in this
place. Be 3D, or at least 4. Throw in all our words for
love, and show up with its face. A 2D lover? Nuh uh.

Everything i love is in between the breaths when you're asleep.
I love you between witticisms.
I love you between global visions.
I love you before the ends you will make meet.
I love you beneath the tweets.
Between the sheets.
I love what i hear between heart

b e a t s .
Because you can google G ∞ d a million times. And I do not fault you if you try. But just this moment, close your eyes. It's closer than this breath. I am closer than this breath. Yes, listen to this breath –

hhhhhhh.

Let it be 3D
Up in this place.
Let's throw in all our names for G ∞ d, and show up
as Its Face.
A 2D life is agony. Knowledge of this is so much
better than tech
knowledge.

•

Fragmentation has
Started
To crystallize
Hard black and white
Crystals of some
Superficial
Imbalance that precipitate
The cloud
To rain
And I am a body
Shaking
Wet
And out of place
In Egypt

Slaves
Walk over me.

Forgive the depth of your longing.

You are the love made to fill it.

I almost died. and I didn't. so I
must. be. alive.

I *must* be alive!

I have breath. It's got me.

It's got me.
Hhhh.

•

LIFTING SADNESS

There may be a bundle of
sadness
abandoned for some
time
in the pit of your stomach or
beneath your left ribs.
So much of your debt has been spent running
distraction from it.
Time spent dancing on the floor above it.
Inward taxes been spent moving to
neighborhoods more lamplit.
To the upper chest side
where breath is shallow and everything follows.

Go to it.
The bundle.
Funny thing is, as soon as you stop distraction, you
will hear it, a crying singularity, crystal in the night.
See me, squeeze me. Breathe into me. Lift it near your heart.
The baby is freezing. Your heart is all the warmth it
needs.
Hand patting its back and bouncing rhythmically:
You are what you are. I am here to love you and see.

Y o u

Have not been abandoned.

TAUGHT • RABBIT

All the men I ever loved:
I want to leave you
In a room

With a lot of
Bright light

So you can put
Strong, so large
Palms on each
Other's swollen
Shoulders that make
The other
Croon in a way
Mine can't.
Fierce foxes to my
Taut rabbit.

Let it all really out
Until I hear a laughter
Through walls and
Know the tears
Have fallen.

I'll come in with
Kombucha
And we'll
All smile so
Warm

Knowing every
Chamber to
Be Home.

We'll imagine for a moment
We can stay and
Start a farm.

And nothing, with me,
Could ever go
Wrong.
She will sing to us
And make us tea.

Then, she'll remember
Not to be a mother
Except maybe one to
herself, but
Keep quiet as
A cold enters
The neck.
You never learned
How to take care of
Me.

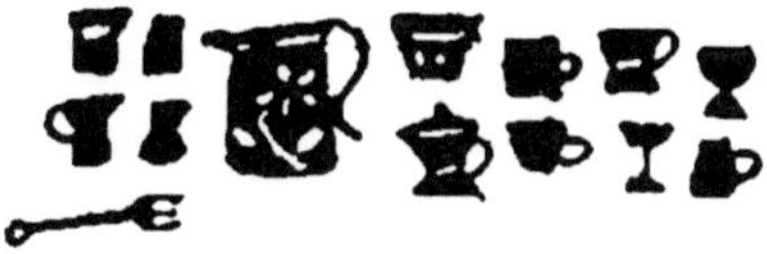

A soft glow from
Behind lights up your eyes.
I feel flutters of
Dash'ed wings.
A battalion of
The most glorious
Singing. It's them.
Oh, they've come. I
Called so many times,
All the ones who've
Ever loved you who
Use my body
To make love to you
When I give them
Room.
I know the way
They love you and
I love them for it.
I know them the most intimately.
From inside myself.

Hello.

I turn to greet
Their brands of
Sunset.
Your lovers. Your mother.
It melts me.

We could stay

Here just
Like this
And be a
Family.

Yes we are
Safe here
Just like this
We,

This family

Tree.

S H O N E

In this Universe, we've made up a tiny portrait
of how things are and should be. I should have a
partner, I need money, I should have vacation, I need
a job. We've made up all of those words, concepts,
and their opposites - 'singledom,' 'poverty,' 'work!'
called them Reality, now pray to the forces of
Universe (in those made up words) to bring them,
change them, manifest them! We rail against this
thing we call Reality when it does not go our way.
Our picture of what is good and bad, what we don't
want and desperately want is within a little basement
room, in a castle, with a
Host that wants to share with us
Everything.
Soften story.
Let yourself be
Shown.
We are being trolls making ridiculous demands in a
cellar of the most majestic kingdom. Stay o p e n to
what is
T r u e . Everything that
We Are.

ANGER'S LULLABY

Here, all of you
Are included.
I am speaking
To you, anger.
And your scowl
Will not turn me into you.
Stick out your tongue
So I can hold it for you and
Silence
Can be
And you'll have
The rest
I can see by your
Eyes you
Need.
That's right, baby
Tears are fine
Give them to me
You've been

Working Such a
Mighty Long Time.

What is the sound of ecstasy?

The distance between
Who I think I should be,
Who I'm afraid I am,
Who I am.

That tape measure.

Collapsing.

•

G l i s t e n to yourself .

Let there be light, and you are light.

NO REJECTION

There is no
Rejection in our dance of
Love.
I just aim to trace the
Inside of the Infinite's face
Lovingly enough to follow Its
Trail and love you enough
To tell you
What I see
From
Inside.

•

There are no such thing as break ups.
Only breakthroughs.

FROM THE MIRROR

Rather than trying to recognize myself

I live the being
Peering out at me
Today

•

This is not "you now."
It's just you,
Just Now.

- *snowflake*

HOR-MOANING

Hor-

mones

Cry

Wolf.

Hormony

Begins with listening and not believing them.

How old are you?

Love does not age,

she said.

GLASS HOUSE

Cry
Until you say
Oh G ∞ d accidentally
out of pain.

Laugh until you cry.

And love
until you say
Oh G ∞ d accidentally
and so loudly it
makes your partner
laugh.

These are the
Portals.

The windows
In this house
Made entirely
Of
Glass.

WE ARE NOT WOMEN

Thank G ∞ d
We are not competition
But Women.

Thank G ∞ d we are not women
But Human.

Thank G ∞ d we are not human
But

Love.

•

I don't believe in muggles.

I was absolutely sure. The end of Harry Potter would, of course (!) be when we find out that there is no such thing as a muggle. That every being has magic in it, and a wizard is one who is aware of hers. The Highest Wizard, though, (presumably Harry Potter) is the one whose power is to recognize each person's magical power within them, even as they themselves are unaware of it. He was to be the one who saw the magic in everyone and in so doing awaken their dormant power and make It known! Majesty, indeed!

Instead they all got married. And used their magic to walk through walls.

I guess it's for us to finish.
I guess it's for us to
W a l k.

We are the ones who see the magic in everyone and in so doing awaken their dormant power and make It known!

Seat 2B

You are the one we've been waiting for .

On the plane and late after a long good-bye.

Alice! The flight attendant exclaimed as I approached. The whole plane had been waiting for Alice, and here I apparently was.

An extra long good-bye, I explained.

As I took to my assigned seat, the ego-mind entertained the possibility that there were people on the plane thinking,

Well, if that's Alice it was well worth the wait.

She was worth waiting for.

Mind catches itself, *No,* it shadowboxes, defending its ungraceful blurt of arrogance,* *Not because I'm beautiful but maybe I was so lovely, pleasant- glowing, even, upon entering.* I might have cracked more of a joke. *What if I had?* It says. I could have thanked everyone for waiting like a big announcement. My little Extra-Long-Good-bye comment was sweet, but not a big laugh. And probably even made Someone angry- *You have love, so we wait?*

Hmmm. Not beauty, or wise glow, or humor. The mind searches like a computer scanning for worth. What made me worth waiting for? What makes me worth waiting for? Not that they should have left, but how have I made up for the

delay?

Then something dawns on me.

I am Alice.

Who cares? Who's that? The mind can say.

The one assigned to 18F. Alice is the One Who They Were Waiting For. I am Alice, and I am simply here to take a seat. To fill the emptiness assigned that name.

I am Alice. And here I am. No song and dance. I have arrived, and the fact of my being here is all there is or ever was. I needn't say a thing, do a thing, think a thing, or be a thing. I am Alice, and no one else will do.

There is a space for your being. If not filled by you it will go empty and a whole collection of Being will be kept waiting, not knowing just what for.

Arrive in gratitude that you've made it, and take a seat.

You are you, and no one else will do.

Welcome.

****what is called "arrogance" by the mind which takes itself far too seriously, is really just a thought with the selfsame root as the one that says "I'm not good enough." All to be held so softly. Thoughts are not for sorting, but parting - like a window curtain - to see through.***

The infinite doesn't need you

But to be
Visible on
This earth.
You need nothing
But it's Good when your legs
Listen when you want to walk!
And that's the way it is.
G ∞ d is good. Set!
And from your very insides it is saying to the leg we are
Carry me
Out.
Execute compassion for that one there. See, yes,
Over there in that corner.
I know it's a dark night
But you are the
Way
I can help.

•

W O R T H

We rescue the child
Worth
From every burning house
The mind perceives
It all is.
We are drenched in
Sweat and in constant
Alert having
Run the streets in
Darkness following
Cries of
Distress.

It is dawn.
The time to follow
Delight.

The fire was a nightmare
A nightmare is just a dream

And
You
Are
The

Baby
(Worth)

All grown up.

•

wave-particle duality: fundamental tenet of quantum mechanics that says depending on which type of experiment used, L i g h t will sometimes behave like a particle, sometimes like a wave.

You are not to look to a n y t h i n g external as indication or validation of your worth. This will always lead to trouble. Someone else's behavior is not to be used as barometer of your magnificance. It doesn't work, and how could it? Because probably they didn't sleep the night before, or they get nervous around hot/smart/quiet/awkward/loving/anxious-whatever-you-are people, left their glasses at home and can't see you very well, broke up last week with a blankfriend, had a hard time with boss at work, had a spiritual awakening that they are not nearly ready to put into words, had a friend when they were two years old who scratched their eye and looked a lot like you... *things* stirring, moving, influencing their behavior that are unseen, oftentimes even to them, and most certainly to your self-absorbed mind. It is not self-absorbed in a bad way, that's how minds work! It is just wrong about what's happening for other people because everyone else's mind is equally self-absorbed! It is most often a bit off about what is happening, drawing from a database of options that does not include the other person's downloads and that cannot include what is happening in all its intricacy and brand new possibility, in this moment. The mind is a database of the past. It is the only part of your body with no nerve-endings giving it access to immediate information of what is happening around you right now.

Perfect, shmerfect.

I said ***LOVE***!

Love is not a thin line you need to walk.
If you are holding your breath, sucking in your
tummy, or walking a line,
You have been pulled over by the cops while
intoxicated. And, while perhaps drunk, you are not in
love.
Rather than a tightrope,
Love is a floor, beneath you, unconditionally e x p a n
s i v e .
It is the foundation of your very being.
Stop juggling behaviors and
Gracefully exit the circus. ∞

•

NO MORE

No more pretending
You are not the
Sky.

No more pretending
You don't hurt.

No more pretending anything
Can possibly hurt
You.

No more holding back tears.

Rain is.

You offer what only the
Sky
Can.

Sound out

Ssshhh

THE OPPOSITE OF ME

You're on a street
Running east and west and
You know that you're eastbound,

Then the street intersects with those parallel
And you know that you're
Falling Down.

No, there's no going straight forever.

Know that
Movement and change
Are the rules.
You try your best to block out the weather
And then realize you don't have the tools.

So you're soaked to the bone and
You're shaking.
You think
This time its won and I'll die.

Somewhere in you is glad not to be faking
Finally not driving it's your time
To Fly.

I never buy cars
I just rent them
That way they're not mine
So I'm never attached.
My flesh body and I
Get to be soul then
Driving steel bodies that
Live too well
Not to get scratched.

So I drive like the wind
It's just the me and the road
I just try not to
Reap more out of life
Than I've sowed.
I look left I look right when
I'm stopped at a light
Some say eye contact's dangerous
And I hope that they're right cuz
I've come here to struggle
I'm armored to fight
I actually refuse to talk to
No one
Tonight.

Somewhere I'm aware of going south and
Don't mind.
If I go that way long enough I'll find that
I've climbed.
Who is it who found out
You laugh when you cry?
You must go down to go up
Succeed
When you don't try.
And all colors reflected all add up to
White
So One might have suspected that we'd get it right.

Truth
Lives in the crack between
What's white and what's black.
Discovery's found between opinion and fact.
Growth happens to us
When there's no light around
Freedom of mind
Comes
When our bodies are bound.

Ask Galileo, Balzano-

They touched Infinity
When they sat
In confinement
Maybe
Pain
Was
The
Key.

Did they know that they'd
Fly there or
Did they ask
Why? G ∞ d why?
Did they feel
So
Alone
There
While they discovered
The Sky?

And I
Give thanks
To the
alice
Who's the opposite
Of me
Who lives on the
Other side of the globe.
She's pro-war

She's quite shy,
She cuts down big trees
But just like me in some ways,
I'm told.
She's pulling a rope on her side
of the world.
I get up every morn to
Pull mine.
If she took a day off, well,
I'd never wake up.
People would go to my funeral,
Say it was My Time.

The end .

Is also .

The Beginning .

Every time .

•

LYING UNDER

I am the goddess who has
Hated the word "Goddess," and
So hugs you tighter when you
Roll your eyes at it.

I know.

There is nothing here for you to think, understand, or agree with.

I giggle glee every
piss, breath, whistle of
Tea-kettle and sob.
It is all the same to me. Let it out!

I am the goddess who
Pours herself into this
Spherical moment and
Cracks it like an
Egg to gush down
Your leg until you
Surrender to the goo
And then I lick it up.

Your eyes roll back in
a new way this time-

all by themselves.
•

And I am she who will not
leave you with a wet
ankle even when you
brush it off.
"You're fine."

I see you there, in those eyes
Far from it and
within that I see it-
The You that today you've
forgotten you are.

Our hearts press in on one another
and a shock happens like
emergencies at hospitals
and I whisper "clear"
And everything becomes
Such.

I am the goddess to surrender
To for I am you and it has
Nothing to do with "we."

Clearing wants to happen through bodies.
Oh my G ∞ d there is so
Much love for you, not of me (not mine), I have not
Even known you. Just
So much you pouring through this body that
Begs to return to yours.' So, ha, let it.
Let it in and up and OW.
You are home, baby.
And everything
You've ever and
Never could have
Dreamed.

You are everything you've been searching for.
In every goddess who's passed by.
You've hated them, the word, even, and so rolled your eyes.

You've hated them for holding on to so much of you.

I am the goddess who offers it all back.
I relinquish you back to
Your home.

Hold it gently and
Take good care
So it might not
Run away
Again.
And so together our eyes
Can roll back in permanent
Ecstasy, having shed
Their teenage tendencies.
Oh, this is we,
All grown up.

Sluff off your story.
I beg you leave
It at the
Door
Unfold your limbs
Like the midwife
Would if you'd been
Born as supported
As you are here
In my
Heart.
Ha, you say. Shut up. Embarrassed.
Lash out.

Yes. I say to you
Yes, and every single
Word and
Wound.
Swing, swing hard and
Break
Down,
Or
Play
Cool.
Ssssssssshhhhh.

It is hot in here.

The bed is made for
Every one.
All the yous that came with you.
It's a party and I have
Arm for every one.
And they, a hole that I see full
Now
And instantly.
Not by my hand
But by what is and
Could never be
Otherwise.

I'm the one who doesn't
Want to be understood
Cuz it's all
Blah blah anyway.
Any word any one can say.

I'd love to see that
Look on your face, though, the moment
Of
Understanding the Underlying
While lying under me:

That there is no
Such thing

As falling.
You are low as
You can go
(As you somewhere suspected.)
And so you are
Grounded and
Supported
Unconditionally and
All the time.
Ah ha, you say
Ah ha. Somewhere
(as tears come)
maybe I knew,
you say. I think
I knew. -

I am the goddess that
Don't stop when I
Should.
You get it already.
But I don't need
I just want and
That makes me here
More
Cuz want has no
Ceiling. So we can see the
Sky.

Get Naked!

I say when you walk through the door.
Leave every article of
News,
Judgement, insult, compliment-
Newsworthy glory and failure and what they called you
at work today over a cup of worth they keep threatening
to take away.
Who are you without that hat?
Drop your clinging to the past though it is quite cute.
Leave your father's house and
Come into my rooms.
These arms and
Thank G ∞ d
Your heart
Your heart,
Love, is more
Than he could
Ever ever
Do.

•

SUCH GOOD QUESTIONS

The only true knowledge comes of surrender.
And as long as I am a finite being, I find I cannot
surrender silently,
though constantly I do.

I offer this Heart within the machine pounding in this
chest.
I offer the lifebreath of this blood. I offer the ocean that
includes the taste within the buds of this tongue. I see
through every set of eyes. I offer it to that i. every thought
I offer to the current of these waters. I offer this breath to
the sound within the beginning of the breath that is in a
body across oceans within the Ocean.

I am consumed.
Amoeba and everything, all.
I, the I, the I, the i.

Who is it swimming in you, but You, Yourself?

There is pain when I think it must be supposed to be
different. We are supposed to know what You, we, I, All- is.

There is fear when I think of forgetting.

I offer the love that made that fear and the forgiveness of
forgetting.

I offer it back. I offer it back. I offer it back to I.

I am that I am.

I swim in i.

Sssssssssssshhhhhhhhhh...

She will rest, she who has written.
She is asleep.

I and we are love.
That is her secret.
That she keeps from
herself.
So that she can keep
asking such good
questions
And make an offering of
her
Life.

•

G ∞ D SCENT*

Traversing the
Terrain of
These 4 Worlds
With Grace
Is to have less
Preference
For which one
Is dwelled in.
The kind of love
That is Mastery
Of each so much
That the heart
Cares not the
Name and qualities
Of its immediate
Lover
For love is love

And G ∞ d is all and
Scent is a part
Of each

I shall follow my
Nose
Back to you with

Yes.

Yes

to every world
You create.

I love you even when
You are not naked

That's what unconditional

Love is
And you are teaching
Me so well how
To be
You.

Though it is killing me.
G ∞ d knows.

•

**scent- the last sense left after leaving body. The sense corresponding to the highest world. The garden of eden.*

N a k e d   r e s c u e s

~ I t ~ back. The muchness in madness.
Softness saves all your suchness, and banishes sadness.
Even as it makes room for each fleeting feeling,
Making each so welcome, there can't help but be healing.

Feel the mask of the face- all polite and so pretty.
Melt into your ancient - no more smile. No witty.
M e l t i n g eyeballs in sockets,
The tongue in its mouth.
The lips rendered speechless, the corners go south.

The eye sockets, too, can in this moment use balm.
Press the heels of the hands deep into their calm.
Actually, a c t i v e l y ,
Right now give them that. Paralyze the optic nerve,
let the bright light go black.
Your amazing eyes, so active and listening
can surrender to love.
Their essence. Their glistening.

Surrender all holding. This moment's your mattress.
Let it all charge into Infinity's address. ∞

Leonardo's rumored
Practice
All to preserve the holy
Chalice.
The contents of
Holy G r a i l ,
Y o u Are I t
.

Do not spill the softness .
Your divine
N u d i t y .
Your N a k e d
Dive-in-ity . ∞

•

Hero's Journey

What if -

we remember that the Hero's Journey is real.

What if we shout, *Cut!* from within the scene?

An actor, directing.

A dreamer, waking from within the dream?

I am Indiana Jones. I am in the snake pit. And suddenly

Knowing

that facing snakes is just this part of the story.

Just the part of the story that we are in.

The part in which we happen to

Find

Ourselves.

P r e g n a n t

That's the planet for now,
going about her life, going
to school and getting
crushes and blowing
boys in the backseat and
everything is feeling like
a very big deal like when
her mother dies, and big
buildings blow up and
the government did it,
and some say that they
didn't but then who is the
government, and it's all
very important and the
TVs are bright and bigger
than atlantis, and it's
all very important - but
underneath it ALL... we're
p r e g n a n t .'

PLAY WITH ME

fill it out, like an expectant and becoming fifth grade girl,
done with the flat world
ready for something to be touched by, through,
as.

play with me,

she knows it will be different with she, than the girls
pressed up against the dance floor walls. she can feel
glistening in her eyes. she feels the darkness' magic. she
loves G ∞ d already, though she is patient.
the moment nipple contacts
cup
of the longing she is waiting to embody,
she finds it is not the cup. it is not the breast. it is not the
beauty. it is the feminine presence coursing through her
blood that is called by her name sometimes, and she is
awed, knowing it is everyone. the very one. and ravishes
the body she is beckoned to inhabit.
hot.

what walks in me heats me drowning. it is i only for i've
given everything to it, including my name.
it cannot say embody me, any longer.

i am inside It and wearing its clothes.
don't listen to these words. feel me. if this body
explodes, don't cry. explosion is the edge of longing
surpassed. if only, if only, we are, will be the burning
bush. take the heat - like the bomb canister beside the
western wall.

Let's endure it. let me endure and live through the heart
of your light. roasted by , eaten by, wide opened by you.
which way, i care not. i trust you will have me your way
- the way that it happens is yours'. always. always.

G ∞ d's will is the unraveling. we are not the thread, the
story, the unfolding little thruline of consequence. i am
the naked body. i am the hand. i am undone by all that
is i. i am what happens. i am the lover. i am open to
everything.

kill me.

**a response to Rilke's Book of Hours, Page I, 59*

THEY ASK FOR LOVE

Last night
I could not dance.
My shoulders were
Held
Ransom.
I bought them back
With some
Foolish flopping frolic
That sent the thieves
Out
Laughing into the
Night.
Whatever works.
There's a note hung on every moment.
And on each, a different
Demand.
We have your Life.
To get it back
You'll have to...
In exchange for our
Stolen dance
They're usually demanding us
Dance!

If it is Life we're
Missing
They say
"Live."
And
For the kiss they stole
They ask for L o v e .
Clever little
Beggars.

•

Hereby Life (G ∞ d, Your Self, and I) keeps Itself A l i v e.

ASKED

Life
Likes
To
Watch
Until
Asked
To
Play.

•

TIME ALONE

Ah ha!

G ∞ d is being polite

Giving me time Alone

To do His work.

•

Every moment is in competition with the last. To become the most amazing teacher, an even better teacher. So that this might happen, some teachings of a teacher a year ago, a minute ago, a moment ago, may need to fade and be proven ineffective and so we might be alert to the teachings of the even better far superior most glorious teacher that is

NOW!

When G ∞ d is near whatever and however that could
Possibly not be
Poetry gets Naked
It drops word
And pours out Essence.
It feels sometimes like creativity
Has gone away.
I say, in reverence of the
Closeness
Of the
Creator.

You cannot
Be
Alone.

The neck. Eyeballs.
In the mouth.
The places i am touching with N o w .

- Presence .

TO TREMBLING

This raucous party of bed bouncing and
people getting hurt.

Laughter that turns to tears

Ideas of
what needs
what should
what wants to
happen-
What is WAN-TED (!),

Fall off the bed when the goddess of
What Is
Walks in.

She lays down her naked body in divine ecstasy and
Needs no favors to set the
World to trembling.

•

H u m a n n e s s

Playing catch up after getting stuck in the honey of
eternity.
i walk with G ∞ d's ejaculate still inside me.
So still within it.

Oh, Seed,

Have planted some blueprint of what you wish to see.

Remind me the D r e a m
that upon hearing
the world awakes
to

S e e i n g

•

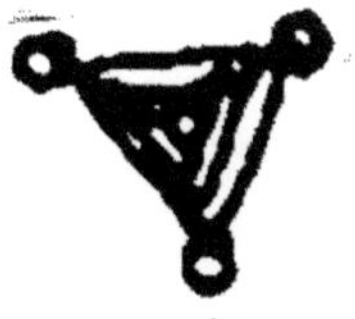

We've been made to handle what's happening.
And what's happening is made for us to
Handle.

(What is happening is made to change us, and we were
made to change what is happening.)

WHY HE TRUSTS ME

I keep giving my me to G ∞ d.

Lately He's been giving me
Back,

Saying,

Make art
Make love
Make something of yourself,

And so i hold the me, a
Ball of
Clay in these
Hands.

Thank goodness
I know they are
G ∞ d's.

Maybe that's why he trusts me.

•

FROM YOUR CLOUD

Do not hear watchdogs inside the Greatest Gifts and
Run.

You have been treasured. And those treasures have fallen
From your darkest cloud
Like rain.

Keep out your tongue.
Life is not finished
Showering
Its most
Beloved
One.

Feel it on the lids of your eyes.

Let go of the pendulum.
The clock will again strike
Now.

•

ASK THE DEAD

Ask the dead to cry us so we might mourn them.
Through these bodies come their tears
Mourning their bodies.

WHAT TO DO

What's so sad about
Waking alone,
When the air on your cheeks
is teeming
in miracle
.
Who is the
Melancholy
Come to visit?
The shadow
of the idea
in legos someone's
built
in
your
brain
that the bed you're
in
is
"Double."

STRADDLE!!!

Your Lover is
Everywhere
Here.
And knows
More even
Than you

What to
Do.

•

Every letting go is a re-aquaintance with eternity.

Keep going,
Love
.

C R Y

Allow grief to escape from us

And we will not have need to
Escape from grief.

Cry.

•

YOU NEEDN'T

I am not saying that
It is easy.
I am only saying
That you needn't
Resist the difficulty.

•

L o v e   w i n s ,

Yes. But for now... Love whines. Winces, whimpers
- but only for a moment. Like the moment Jesus on
the cross, so sturdy that all is Divine Will, suddenly
dipping underneath saying "Oh, WHY have you
forsaken me." Forgetting All is That and plunging
seconds into
h u m a n i t y . Ow.
Then love wines the little s/he, the me, winning we.
Coaxing me back into solidarity. The clarity of Unity
within everything. To be We. To be S h e . To be the
solution. To say *Hineini.* To say ' Hello darkness, I have
known you before and I will not fall for your disguise
of Other.'
It be your job to juice me, shedding fibrous
complacency, shackles made of the unsuspected angels,
Ease and Decency. Having evacuated, here we are to
find light in what we're left with.
Level 12 of an old arcade. Can you widen your heart
to contain this stage? Love so impossibly inseparably?
Love wins because we're playing. Love wins for we
remember the game. To see self in all apparent enemies
and Be, unshakably infinite. And not for once, the
same.

Wins. Whines. Whimpers. Wines. Whispers.
Witnesses. Love Wins.
You're It. ∞

•

Love first.

We wait for an indication of love to come from an external source. Somebody across the table from us. Somebody in the room. To hug first. To say that's what the protocol is here. If you do it, it becomes the protocol.

Love first. Create that connection. Create that opening.

And it all pours in.

We do the same thing when we show up in any religious setting, spiritual setting, yogic setting. We go to our mat and we wait there for G ∞ d to prove something to us. Show me, show me that you are here. Show me something. Prove something. Life, prove something to me- that you're worth living.

It won't.

It won't prove itself to you. You have to love first. Show up loving, loving, loving. That will open your heart.

Only then, when your heart is open, can you feel the love that is all around you.

That has always, always, always been there.

Always.

The love that you are, so innately, so deeply.

It's all right there,

Contained in the people around you. Contained in the air around you and inside yourself. Your heart must be open to even receive it. Even notice it. It is there.
Love first.

How much different

spending life making sure you don't die alone might be, from making sure no one does.

- *Community.*

- *Uniamory.*

Darkness has purpose. That we cultivate our inner compass.
We were made to do this. Thank you for
S e e i n g
Us through
This.

•-

If Penetration is re-m e m b e r-ance. Withdrawal is
forgetting. It is in the back and forth that L o v e is
Made.
L i f e . (i love you)

Y O U . A R E . T H A T .

∞

Don't be sorry.
Live up to yourself.
Don't prove a n y t h i n g .

•

Don't surrender.
Except to whatever's happening.
Even to this little string of
Words who have never met you
But love you
And
Know you
And what is best-
You

•

You need not be the wizard.
You, you are the magic.

When you don’t try to be cool, you’re warm.

That’s hot.

It came into the space between us the
Moment i looked into your eyes.
And I swallowed it into me and found
It already knew me inside.

I wondered why didn't anyone tell me that i would know love without a doubt. You don't ask *could this be pain* when someone blows you upside the head. I never asked, *could this be joy* when a smile danced across my face. I didn't have to ask What It Was when your p r e s e n c e filled my

Space .

We're given this word to play with.
" L O V E "
is this mysterious noun.
We're thrown into our lives, no idea of what it looks like,
can i touch it?
Will it make a sound? We're just told that until you find it,
Y O U
Will not be found.
We ask *Could this be it?!* when our tailbones are black and
blue from rocking back and forth because that is what i was
told i was supposed to do.

You
Over there
Dressed in whatever body they put you in
This Time Round,
I've seen what's behind your eyes
And it's pulling me right out of myself.
What i've got in this body,
This body i'm dressed in
This Time Round
Has been waiting to see you again. The
You
I See Right Now.
And i will stand right here in front of you
Encountered by my destiny, asking why didn't anyone
tell me it would be
so . easy .

Like a blow upside the head.

Where did it go?

You tell me.

It's not a challenge

It's just an inquiry.

I don't like sounding desperate but i do like sounding like
What I Am, and i can't help but feel the two of us have
been robbed. Scammed. Because

I am here.

And i need to know. Please. Where did all that go?

It came into the space between us the moment i looked
into your eyes.
And i swallowed it into me.
It's now consumed my insides.
It felt so good to have it there.
We didn't think to ask -

How?

But, love.

Would you look at all the

Space

Between us

Now.

Let your eyes
Fall upon

s p a c e

With no thoughts in their way.

Gaze s o f t

Allowing landscape

To pixelate .

Surrender

The Naming

This *chair*. that

Water

Falling into

Broad strokes

Whereby

All is the

Other.

•

PAIN'S JOB

I cry at the unnecessariness of loneliness,
When we all have infinite hugs to give. ∞
I think that's where pain's intelligence comes in.
It's got a pen in its hand, saying, *This just in,*
The way that we're living is not the given.
Love is a resource pulsating within,
Because it wants to come out toward every human!
(Not something we're running around, desperate to win!)
Get to it, because your hindering flow creates depression.
Dole it out, find its expression!

Pain, with a gasping breath, laying down its pen,
passes the memo named *What Should Be*
through a slot marked *What Could Be,*
And is immediately let go,
(To get a good sleep)
While the staff hustles to print it
Before the dawn of new day

So that it can influence it.

Then the whole staff b r e a t h e s , awed at the wisdom

that was
Just
Received.
Their most treasured consultant, not full-time
employee, Pain.
He's on leave.

I cry seeing
A reflected sunrise in a pair of new
Eyes passing on the street.
You know me. We smile, suddenly not alone.

That constant truth makes me weep. *(You're me)*
Another wise, parched heart.
The dew of love wetting an otherwise parched heart.
Knowing now what that parch meant.
It was all for the interaction of this very moment.

I cry when anyone I'd call *us, my* religion, *my* country
Tis of thus.
Pretends there's a *them* and perpetrates violence.
Tears instruct intelligence- *This is unjust.*
It's funny, my face stays drier when violence is u p o n
the *we,*

117

The tears mostly flow when it's *we* acting violently.
That's how I know, tears are trying to influence me.
The yes, the no way, the new way, where to go.

They say, *Your eyes are clearer since you've cried.*
Now Go and let love s t e e r .

NEIGHBORHOOD KID

When I let Life lead It usually takes me toward Fear
(It's smart like that.)
It seems it has a plan that we two become good friends.
I was resistant at first but lately I've started to concede.
It's Helpful for the times when everyone else is busy and
Fear's the only One available
to
Play.

•

AAAAAHHHHHHHHH!!!

The point is not to stay perfect
It is to
Let Loose
The Perfection in you.

Sometimes you got to
Throw yourself around
A bit.

S O M E H E R E

It's always the end of the world somewhere.

Don't take it TOO personally if it's in your room.

Somewhere, a sun rises so new.

Anew .
In you .

NEW GAME!

Today has
All
New
Rules.

PARTY DOWN

Go easy on
Yourself in
Remembering
That we are
Not these bodies.

It is hard
-Too hard-
To know
The exact
Protocol
As to where
Precisely where to hang them
(these newfangled things!)
Or how to wear them
So that they don't
Drag the whole
Party
Down.

123

I include these things. I am not these things. ∞

I n - v e n t o r y (g e n t l e n e s s)

There is the practice of the Candle. The Feather. We open our inner-most cupboards and take i n - v e n t o r y - Beneath consciousness we hold on before acting, speaking, expressing our Beings- analyzing how it might be taken in, what might people think, what has happened in the past? Has someone said something bad or against what you may do, before? Have you messed up doing it the past? Yikes. All of these factors- most of them having very little to do with this very moment and what is wanted in this particular situation, room, company, nowness. We hold on, not trusting the contents of our own inner-cupboards, pantries, rooms. Our own inventory in the dark places. Who knows what might be in there? How am I to let in guests? How am I to feed of the contents of this being freely, lovingly, with abandon, without self-consciousness, reticence, apology- false humility?

And so we take inventory. Without fear (or including it) we boldly face what is in the corner cupboards. We see it and the space it takes up. We i l l u m i n a t e it with the flame the soul is. ("The human soul is G ∞ d's candle»). And how do we treat it? With the feather. The gentlest touches. No Brillo here, no bleach. Illumination and a softness beyond kindness. A g e n t l e n e s s that bends to anything. A melting. A give. A complete letting go.

The extent to which we can surrender this being and
let through all the action, love, words, silence that
wants through us to express the presence of Truth, of
Shechinah, G ∞ d... is beyond fathomability.
It is what we are called upon here to do. See everything
so we can release, let go, and let the work of the
Feather, through.

LOOK • WHERE • YOU • ARE

Some poems speak from inside a circle.
They say,
"Hey! Look where I am!"
In excited voices they
describe the Splendor of their surroundings!

The wallpaper is just...
And oh, the feast, best yet,
There is no ceiling. This place goes on and on!
We are outside breathing heavy,
leaning on a temple,
Exhausted from searching for a door!
"I'm tired." You say
and listen to their laughter.
(Can't they hear?)
Maybe next lifetime, you say to yourself
In an ant crawling by.
Other poems become doors.
They say come into me,
I'm yours'.
They lay themselves as the circle around your feet.
And listen.
And when word is done, temples lie in their lap, and
They say simply this:

Look where you are.

Stop - Sound this out:

*Hbbbbb*h ∞

Tears are c l u e s . That the ocean inside is being stirred.
A truth unearthed from the body basement.
Going in deep, causing water displacement.
A recognition of an unknown yearning,
Or part of self left for dead, softly returning.

Tears are cues. Cues that there is something to do. You are being moved!
Tears are directives. They say *Pay attention! I am instructing your destiny, play detective.*
We've all heard, to find your purpose, *Follow your bliss.* I think tears can be another breadcrumb leading to for this.
So here it is:
I am in a female body that is up inside its thirties. It doesn't cry when it looks at babies. And very little at weddings.
I cry l i k e a baby, though...
When I contemplate the oneness of humanity.
When I witness someone forgiving an apparent enemy.
When I hear Marianne Williamson speak about almost absolutely anything, or watch a minister pledgeing allegiance in the marriage between life-force and her.
Finally giving her body to its whimsy, saying *Play with me in the way you want me, so we can be the change Y o u wish to see. Take*

me, Here in front of everybody.
Like a gay boy who's never heard the word *gay,*
witnessing *gay marriage* on TV, my heart leaping, eyes
weeping, watching an ordination, only knowing
my passion for that divination, not knowing it was
possible to marry It before a congregation!
Turning inward to G ∞ d saying, *Marry me, we're free!*
We can COME OUT! Open my lips, that my mouth might
declare
Your Glory. ∞
I cry when I tune into the peace within my body's
boundaries.
And know it to be everybody.
It is like New York, if you can make it Here, you
can make it Anywhere.
Actually.

You can keep your ok-cupidry and your ideas on the maximum age a woman can conceive. Don't pretend to know my dreams based on biology. And while you're at it, reflect that for this earth, adoption might be key. Weaving a rainbow family that might be kinder ecologically. I am not this body, though my veins course my own destiny.

If you know another human being who sings a similar song
as me, send them my way. That's called
Community.

If in our song there's harmony, the music makes people
happy,
Our happiness might make us dance.
In dancing, baby may be conceived.
And home, in a land of fellow dancers,
We will happily name it

P e a c e .

Naked Outside

Earth - home
Grass.
Sun.
Skin.
Tree.
Food.

We've made it illegal to be

Human
.

Be(A)ware:

Apartment has the word *apart* in it

(Find earth. Find each other. Live together.)

LOVE SPILLING EYES

I choose the default meeting of our eyes to be so deep that it is the Self that I am seeing. The Unified We. The one and the Only. In seeing that in each other instantly, we arouse again, for the first time even, the knowing of our own divinity. And so Be that in the world so much more easefully.
That is what I'd like it to be with you and me.
In the current moment of our collective energy, we've been downloaded a lot about a compulsive coupling tendency. To race into this world looking for that one to be everything. Who without, you will be left lonely.
Desperately.
So we're desperately searching out the eyes, Are you for me?
So it confuses that simplicity of reminding divinity.
Rather than calling G ∞ d forth, we are unwittingly 'flirting'- which means giving attention to. An act that one who seeks to change the world, let's say, might devote oneself to. Making each one on the planet know he is worth it. You are seen, you are known. You are human, too!
So simply bow down to the depths of each soul, to stir it to surface, the darkness to light.
Without only thinking if we want to fuck them tonight.
And,

Without them only thinking we want to fuck them
tonight.
Because let's face it, if that is what it means to look
a being in the face, then you would divert your eyes
mostly, while you mediate your taste. And then when
you finally find one your mind thinks is tasty, it's
usually the one you walk by really hastily, G ∞ d
forbid they actually know you feel this way.
So all in all, our couple compulsion does not work.
And reserving eye contact for 'flirting' is worse
It is killing us off by our own hands, by suicide, the
depths of a loneliness our nature to love can't abide
by.
So let's free the eye contact! Give it to Truth. The one
that says you are me and i am you.
And with confidence that comes from a tethering to
Oneness, Look fiercely in eyes and
save each other with
Softness.

NIGHT LIGHT

From here I can lick the stars.

From way down, was lifted up
Through penthouse of popularity,
Fame and wealth.*

There was a party going there,
As rumored, but everyone at it
Wanted to leave and asking each other
Where there was to go.

And up was I lifted.

A seagull winked.
I sighed- relief.

And when the crown bumped the Moon,
Off it fell.

She lay down in this eye socket.

So at night I can
Love you.

•

Happiness is love exiting the body.

From vowing
Your eternal
Love

to

Vowing
You're eternal
love.

- paradigm shift

uniamory - *n.* having love for every single being on the planet out of recognition that we are one single being. 2. a literal oneness that, when perceived, renders jealousy impossible (to take seriously). Lit. One love.

Natural Flow -

The natural flow for each of us is to walk down the streets allowing that which we are, a Flow of unconditional love, to pour forth to be received as acknowledgement "hello" of each and every being. This is natural.

Our conditioning within the paradigm of coupleship creates an unnatural hoarding, causing us to hold onto that which we are, this infinite wellspring of Love, eye each person and think - "Am i attracted or not attracted, do I look attractive right now, would that be rejected or received, would it be safe or unsafe, appropriate, not appropriate, what would my girlfriend say if she saw me smile at someone?"

stagnating the flow of energy creating Depression (Happiness is love exiting the body) creating a massive epidemic of Loneliness in our time.

The least efficient and sustainably distributed resource in our time is

our selves, the unconditional love that we are.

A resource that is entirely infinite.

That is why the paradigm of coupleship is failing.

That is why it will not allow itself to be sustained.

Unconditional love is here to be maximized.

We were built for its purposes, not it for ours'.

It is what bodies are for.

CONSPIRACY

Aspiring
To
Rise
To fulfill
Physically the
Love
That
Is

Is an actor
Perspiring to
Fulfill her role,
its eloquence and poetry,
In a Shakespearean play.

The set standing on its
Tip-toes to reach the height
Of its metaphors.

But we are Shakespeare
In the stage structure of
His own play.
We are love
Aspiring

To fulfill
Its own
Perfection

And finding it,
Itself, complete
Upon

Entrance.

There is no performing here.

We are done.
Curtain down.

Eyes

Open

Wide.

Therein, the play is perfect.
And everything, with you,
In you,
My love, is
Play.

I want you to be everyone you want you to be.

L o v e , Simply .

i have so much not to say to you.

I am perfect with zero lovers, for I am w i t h everything.
I am perfect with one lover, for that one is everything.
I am perfect with many lovers, for everything is one.
-U N I A M O R Y-.

Freedom and love are the same.

If you do not feel free, start loving.

PORTRAIT OF PLEASURE

Naturally,
Nothing is not
Child's play.

Sex unfurls its flower
Head and spreads seed on a breeze like
Dandelion

Without planting down dark in the soil
Deep.

We sprout in clusters
Not ones and twos.

With air between
Breathing
Life

Without sucking,
Wilting the one

For the sake of others.

Music is only about everyone's being each other,

And it makes us laugh at once.
And clean up is crayons in a box, and fun.
And all are called into the portrait of pleasure.
There is no confusion of how to smile.
We don't exist.

And you know where my tent is. And I do not leave
Its opening
In the heat of the day I see you
Wherever your body lays.

HOLY EFF

I used to want to make “Holy Fuck” condoms. The slogan would be “Enlighten your Load,” and each condom would come with a (short) prayer, reminder, or affirmation to read.

A pause at the post of the threshold. A *mezuzah.**
Marking the entering of a portal
whispering the name of sweet Oneness as we slip past an apparent duality
Affirming the true Unity as we surrender into the painless Reality of Eternity.
Ecstasy.

We’re already One.
(The act is Bonc-us.)

**A mezuzah is an indicator to stop before you leave a room, and say, “Yes! I am journeying into another room. I am leaving here, but there is nothing Out There that isn’t Right Here. “*
*It is marked with the Shema**- affirmation of the Oneness of Everything. A setting to zero, surrendering into so fully being right here. And so I walk forward for the sake of nothing. It is without intent to get anything. For when I have gathered my Self to this extent, I am Everything.”*
I am playing in the illusion that there are two rooms. Ha!
Within this game, I am at One.

Speak when spoken through.

• ORGANISM •

We are one organism
with millions of orifices
made up to make love
with our existence.

153

(We are one body. it is more arbitrary which
mouth is speaking. Which heart is aching.
Distinctions held more softly. We are one. body.)

Open my lips that my mouth may
be yours.

I don’t want to speak to you,
I move over to be spoken through.
Don’t say ‘embody me,’
i’m in your clothes, conjuring
the dream we wish to see.
the road is You
have the key
ready to be driven
given completely.

Don't listen to the words. Feel me.
Don't cry if this body explodes.
Exploding is longing, surpassed.

Is that the purpose?
to be fully encompassed.
To let the heart beat the drum fast?
To let go and to be danced?

Let me endure it
and sometimes adore it.
If we don't explore it
then what are we here for?

So i will adore it
i will abhor it
i'll feel every emotion
open up to explosion.

Let me live through the heart of your light.
roasted by, eaten by, see through your sight.
Take me. i trust you will have me your way
The way it happens is yours'. Always.

Your feet can never leave holy ground
no matter where the path goes.
Obstacles make your calling clear,

What if it all goes wrong is the delusion of
Fear.

G ∞ d is willing the unraveling.
it is the core of all our traveling.
Witness the story
with a flash of your glory.

Your feet can never leave holy ground
no matter where the path goes.
Obstacles make your calling clear
Wherever you go you're always here

Get tossed so you can know falling
Get lost to know you're always found.
The dead-end is actually a doorway.
Knock before turning around.

Keep keep keep letting go for the next thing that now, you can't possibly know.

Get out the familiar
Leave your father's home
Go to the place that I will show you,
The space you weren't sure was true, before,
Let the mind be blown

What you knew, but hadn't Known.

Life promotes our unraveling.
We are not the thread,
We are not the sweater,
We are G ∞ d naked.

We are not gender, our storyline,
unfolding consequence.
We are one nude body.
Love's luminous omniscience.

•

Physics says, mysteriously, *Light becomes a particle by the Observer asking the question,* ***"Where are you?"***

The first question in the Bible is "Where are you?" just here, after the fruit is eaten. The observer asks Adam and so shrinks him down to a particulate being.

Consciousness is everywhere, evenly. There is no molecule that is not its eye. Omniscience, speaking from Adam's own tongue, is not confused. This is not the kind of "Where are you?" where someone is seeking to find. It is Observer contracting the wave to particle. The all That We Are down to a you, an I. So that we wrap ourselves in earth to cover body from being seen. It's all a dream.
It takes a certain shedding to wake up. A return to Eden. A shedding of the leaves and names. Like you, like me. Like shirt. Like tree.

(What is the question you can whisper to your mind to become your greatest you?
The word mantra means "transport beyond mind." Whatever your answer to this question- This is yours.)

Physics: One, Oh One. One No One.

The Garden of Eden is the experience of pure present consciousness. The utter synchrony of being moved from a space of stillness. A constant quickening from Nothing. You- the mouth, the hands, the tongue of the All. You- a wave.

Physics says, mysteriously, *Light becomes a wave by the Observer asking the question,* ***"Where are you going?"***

Ejection from the Garden, from that pure state of oneness, happened in the story we've all heard, when a fruit was eaten from a tree. Suddenly the humans experience duality. They experience a separation, a "you" and a "me." And a brand new concept called "nudity."

What was a seamless reality became a thought-about partial reality. Once wave, Adam became a particle with limits and boundaries. He cries "I'm naked," and covers himself shamefully. He grabs the leaf from that very tree. It becomes the first fashion piece.

Love. Gratitude. Forgiveness. You. _____.

Synonyms.

What Heraclitus called
The Hidden Harmony
Moses experienced as
a still, small voice
Lao Tsu called the Tao, and
Jesus,
the peace that passeth
understanding.

I call

You.

God.
Then Yom Kippur day, when I was 20 years old.
By myself in my tiny room in New York City.

S o m e t h i n g happened that seriously undermined my quotation marks around *God.* It was completely unsolicited. I was not a spiritual seeker. I didn't even do yoga. And, I was happy. No hitting bottom scenario, here. It was as one who had grown up without a word for "couch," only to one day look down and find that she was sitting on something soft.

Couch. She might say.
Suddenly, a reality so much more different than

T h e   e x p e r i e n c e   .

God. The word freaked me out.
I used to feel softly sorry for people who
thanked it on *Oprah*, or in Playbills. *I just want to
thank G ∞ d.*
Oof, I'd think. *Thought she was smarter than
that. Cooler than that. More sophisticated. Too bad.
Downright embarrassing.* It seemed so *obvious* that
we just don't know a whole lot stuff that we
wish we could know, and if x = the stuff that we
don't know about that we wish we could know,
and x makes us uncomfortable, let's make it
knowable. Let's give it a name! Therefore, x =

to the floor. I sat. on the floor. And I suddenly knew to light a candle. I had never done that before.

My body began to shake. I remember opening my eyes and seeing the flickering of the candle and feeling that the shaking of my body was in sync with its motion. There was a distinct feeling of being spiritually "scalped." I felt a splitting open of the top of my head and rather than bound by my quaking body, I was a matrix of Stillness that was sitting as the nuclei in the zero-points in the web of everything. I was ecstasy. *Oh my God*, I uttered over and over, as it effortlessly, inevitably rolled off my own lips.

another planet might be.

I was sitting on my bed. I'd told my parents I wasn't coming home for the most holy day of the Jewish Year, Yom Kippur. I wasn't feeling it. I'd been inspired by a reading of *The Fountainhead* and was in a period of questioning all forms of religion.

I was being an actor in New York. I was waiting to hear about what would have been my first big role in a film. It had been a seven day wait. Other than that, a normal day. Suddenly, from the center of my solar plexus I felt gravity, like a pull, almost physically taking me down

from nothing. A fish who had not known the
water. An ocean of the opposite of oblivion and
in love

with All.

What is the word for the alarmingly
intoxicating, unified intelligence that we are
swimming in and that swims inside, us all
the time? We can give it a name. We can give
it all
the names. Or not. Here, I do, with so much
love.

This word, formerly so suspect, suddenly a description of the only thing that Was. The only thing that Is.

I remember, after what felt like forever, turning back toward my bed. I looked at the Laura Ashley knock-off, flowered bedspread. *Oh my God,* was uttered immediately, but in a new way this time. This presence that was palpable against each eyeball, was connected from within every cell- was of what the bedspread was made; of what it was all made. *Hello,* I whispered to I in the bedspread.

I was immersed in the pool of One, separate

Us.

G∞d.

You.

•

The door opened a
Crack
to your dark childhood room,
Your call suddenly answered
By the opening of the door.
And there is no dark
But a spark.

Then, well, for the love of that,

Use the word.

A Note on the word 'G ∞ d.'

Forget it.

Forget it.

It is not yours.

Unless when you close your eyes, breathe, and think
god
A little chimney opens from your forehead and your
body begins filling with something that looks a lot like
hallway light streaming in
Suddenly

of my own tongue that I cannot taste for the simple fact that it has never not been in my mouth. This is a recipe for something tasted for its having quickened in me, tongue against roof. It is a way that it is.

•

These are not poems -

A man I know left his wife for another woman.
Before her, when poets spoke of love I didn't believe in it. I'd thought they were being poetic, he said. That is how so much of life is. We have no idea until it's at our door. The words are empty until they're in our own mouths, the thing we'd been staying alive to find, the thing we didn't dare believe in, speaking through us, describing itself. 'I am love. This is what I like.'
This is not poetry. It is description. I am not a poet. I am a field reporter. I am an avid lover

C A U G H T

This is not a poem.

It is ejaculate from G ∞ d
Caught on this page.